REALLY EASY GUITAR

ADELE

22 SONGS WITH CHORDS, LYRICS & BASIC TAB

T0083368

2 All I Ask

4 Chasing Pavements

6 Daydreamer

8 Easy on Me

10 Hello

13 I Drink Wine

16 Love in the Dark

18 Lovesong

20 Make You Feel My Love

22 Million Years Ago

24 Oh My God

27 One and Only

30 Rolling in the Deep

33 Send My Love (To Your New Lover)

36 Set Fire to the Rain

38 Skyfall

40 Someone Like You

42 To Be Loved

48 Turning Tables

50 Water Under the Bridge

45 When We Were Young

52 Woman Like Me

55 GUITAR NOTATION LEGEND

Cover photo © Getty Images / CBS Photo Archive / Contributor

ISBN 978-1-70515-962-0

Visit Hal Leonard Online at
www.halleonard.com

World headquarters, contact:
Hal Leonard
7777 West Bluemound Road
Milwaukee, WI 53213
Email: info@halleonard.com

In Europe, contact:
Hal Leonard Europe Limited
42 Wigmore Street
Marylebone, London, W1U 2RN
Email: info@halleonardeurope.com

In Australia, contact:
Hal Leonard Australia Pty. Ltd.
4 Lentara Court
Cheltenham, Victoria, 3192 Australia
Email: info@halleonard.com.au

All I Ask

Words and Music by Adele Adkins, Bruno Mars, Chris Brown and Philip Lawrence

(Capo 4th Fret)

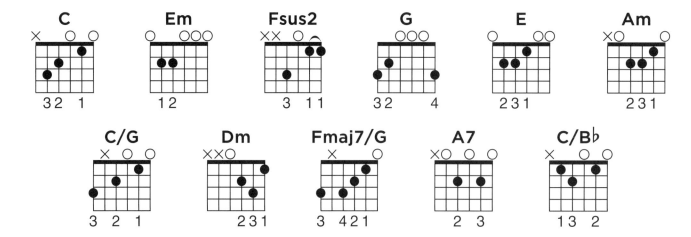

INTRO

Slow

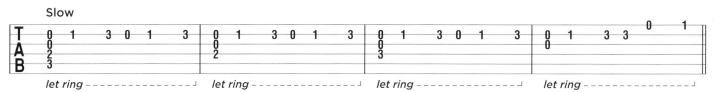

let ring ---------------   let ring ---------------   let ring ---------------   let ring ---------------

VERSE 1

C   Em
I will leave my heart at the door.

   Fsus2   G
I won't say a word. They've all been said before, you know,

   C   Em
so why don't we just play pretend like we're not

Fsus2   G   E
scared of what is coming next or scared of having nothing left.

PRE-CHORUS

   Am   C/G   Dm Fmaj7/G
Look, don't get me wrong, I know there is no tomorrow. All I ask is

CHORUS 1

C   A7   Dm Fmaj7/G   G
if this is my last night with you, hold me like I'm more than just a

C   A7   Dm Fmaj7/G   G
friend. Give me a memory I can use. Take me by the hand while we

C G Am   Dm   Fmaj7/G
do what lovers do. It matters how this ends, 'cause what if I never love a -

INTERLUDE

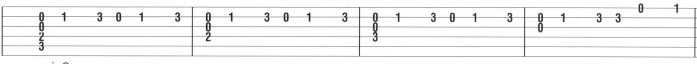

gain?

VERSE 2

C   Em
I don't need your honesty,

    Fsus2   G
it's already in your eyes and I'm sure my eyes, they speak for me.

C   Em
No one knows me like you do

      Fsus2   G   E
and since you're the only one that mattered, tell me who do I run to?

REPEAT PRE-CHORUS

REPEAT CHORUS 1

BRIDGE

C/B♭   F Em Dm   Fmaj7/G G   Em
gain. Let this be our lesson in love, let this be the way we remember us.

      E   Am   Dm   Fmaj7/G
I don't wanna be cruel or vicious and I ain't askin' for forgiveness. All I ask is

CHORUS 2

C   A7   Dm Fmaj7/G   G
if this is my last night with you, hold me like I'm more than just a

C   A7   Dm Fmaj7/G   G
friend. Give me a memory I can use. Take me by the hand while we

C   G Am   Dm   Fmaj7/G
do what lovers do. It matters how this ends, 'cause what if I never love

a - gain?

Chasing Pavements

Words and Music by Adele Adkins and Francis Eg White

(Capo 3rd Fret)

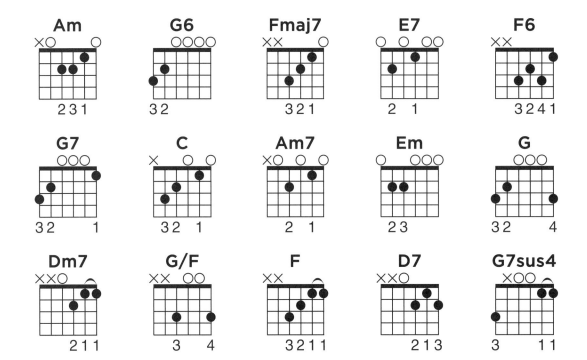

INTRO

Moderately

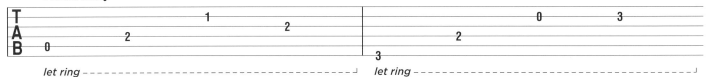

let ring

let ring

VERSE 1

    Am   G6
I've made up my mind, don't need to think it over;

    Fmaj7   E7
if I'm wrong I am right, don't need to look no further.

    F6   G6 G7   C   Am7   Em
This ain't lust. I   know this is love.   But if

C   G   Am
I tell the world, I'll never say enough 'cause it was not said to you,

       E7   Fmaj7 G6 G7
and that's exactly what I need to do if I'd end up   with you.

CHORUS 1

| Fmaj7 | | Em | Am | Dm7 | | Fmaj7 | | G/F | Em | | E7 |
Should I give up?   Or should I just keep chasing pavements even if it leads nowhere?

| Fmaj7 | | Em | Am | Dm7 | | Fmaj7 | | G/F | | E7 |
Or would it be a waste even if I knew my place? Should I leave it there?

| Fmaj7 | | Em | Am | Dm7 | | Fmaj7 | | G/F | Em | | C |
Should I give up?   Or should I just keep chasing pavements even if it leads nowhere? Oo, oo.

VERSE 2

| Am | | G6 |
I build myself up and fly around in circles,

| Fmaj7 | | E7 |
waiting as my heart drops and back begins to tingle.

| F6 | | G6 | G7 |
Finally, could this be it? Or

CHORUS 2

| Fmaj7 | | Em | Am | Dm7 | | Fmaj7 | | G/F | Em | | E7 |
Should I give up?   Or should I just keep chasing pavements even if it leads nowhere?

| Fmaj7 | | Em | Am | Dm7 | | Fmaj7 | | G/F | | E7 |
Or would it be a waste even if I knew my place? Should I leave it there?

| Fmaj7 | | Em | Am | Dm7 | | Fmaj7 | | G/F | Em | | C |
Should I give up?   Or should I just keep chasing pavements even if it leads nowhere? Yeah.

BRIDGE

| F | | Em | | Dm7 | G7 |
Should I give up? Or should I just keep chasing pavements even if it leads nowhere?

| Fmaj7 | | E7 | | D7 | G7sus4 |
Or would it be a waste even if I knew my place? Should I leave it there? Should I   give up?

| Fmaj7 | Em | Am | Dm7 | | F |
Or should I just keep on   chasing   pavements?

| Em | | Am | | Dm7 | | F | F6 | G7 |
Should I just keep on   chasing   pavements? Oh.

REPEAT CHORUS 1

Daydreamer

Words and Music by Adele Adkins

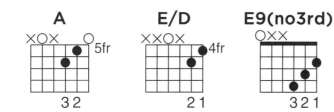
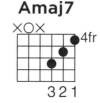
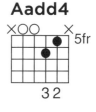
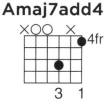

INTRO

Moderately

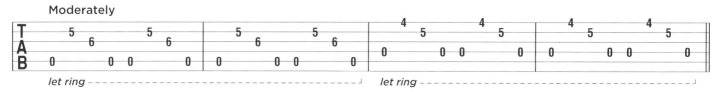

VERSE 1

A
Daydreamer sitting on the sea, soaking up the sun. He is a

E/D
real lover of making up the past and feeling up his girl like he's never felt her figure before.

REPEAT INTRO

VERSE 2

A
A jawdropper, looks good when he walks, is the subject of their talk. He would be

E/D
hard to chase, but good to catch and he could change the world with his hands behind his back, oh.

INTERLUDE 1

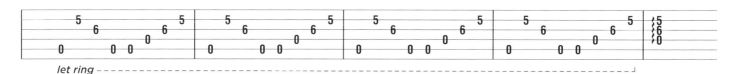

let ring

CHORUS

    E9(no3rd)   **Amaj7**
You can find him sitting on your doorstep,

E9(no3rd)   **Amaj7**
waitin' for the suprise.

    E9(no3rd)   **Amaj7**
And he will feel like he's been there for hours,

    E9(no3rd)   **Amaj7**
and you can tell that he'll be there for life.

VERSE 3

A
Daydreamer, with eyes that make you melt, he lends his coat for shelter. Plus, he's

E/D
there for you when he shouldn't be, but he stays all the same, waits for you, then sees you

INTERLUDE 2

let ring - ⌐   *let ring* - ⌐
through.

BRIDGE

A   E/D
There's no way I could describe him.

A   E/D
What I've said is just what I'm hoping

INTERLUDE 3

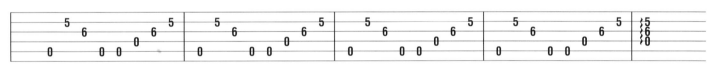

let ring - ⌐
for.

CHORUS 2

   E9(no3rd)   Amaj7
But I will find him sitting on my doorstep,

E9(no3rd) Amaj7
waitin' for a suprise.

   E9(no3rd)   Amaj7
And he will feel like he's been there for hours,

   E9(no3rd)   Amaj7
and I can tell that he'll be there for life.

rit. E9(no3rd)   Amaj7add4
And I can tell that he'll be there for life.

Easy on Me

Words and Music by Adele Adkins and Greg Kurstin

(Capo 5th Fret)

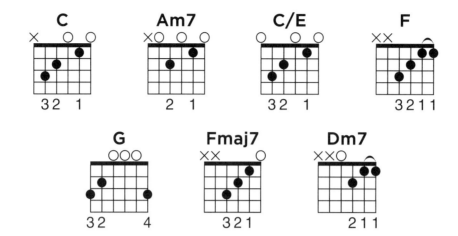

INTRO

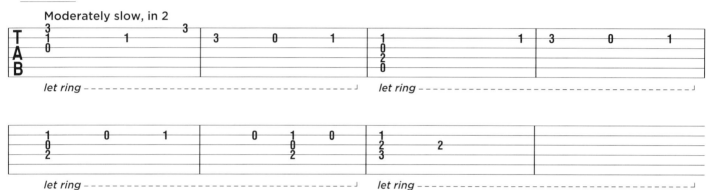

VERSE 1

           C   Am7
There ain't no gold in this river

               C/E   F
that I've been washing my hands in forever.

            C   Am7
I know there is hope in these waters,

            G   F
but I can't bring myself to swim when I am drowning in this

Fmaj7   F Fmaj7
silence, baby. Let me in.

CHORUS 1

```
        C  Am7  G          C/E
Go eas   -   y on me, baby.

        Dm7        C      F
I was still a child,   didn't get the chance to

C    Am7      G
feel      the world around me.

 C/E   Dm7          C        F
I had no time to choose  what I chose to do,

        C            Am7  C/E  F
so go easy on me.
```

VERSE 2

```
            C           Am7
There ain't no room for things to change

            G                      F
when we are both so deeply stuck in our ways.

    C                   Am7
You can't deny how hard I've tried.

    G                  Fmaj7              F  Fmaj7
I changed who I was to put you both first, but now I give up.
```

CHORUS 2

```
        C  Am7  G          C/E
Go eas   -   y on me, baby.

        Dm7        C      F
I was still a child,   didn't get the chance to

C    Am7      G
feel      the world around me.

 C/E   Dm7          C        F
I had no time to choose  what I chose to do,

    C  Am7  C/E         F
So eas  -  y       on me.
```

BRIDGE

```
C                    Am7              G
I had good intentions      and the highest hopes,

            Fmaj7                         F
but I know right now       it probably doesn't even show.
```

REPEAT CHORUS 1

Hello

Words and Music by Adele Adkins and Greg Kurstin

(Capo 1st Fret)

Em	G/D	D	C	Bm	G
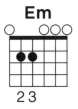		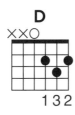	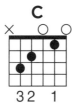	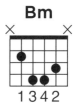	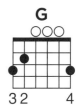
2 3	4	1 3 2	3 2 1	1 3 4 2	3 2 4

INTRO

Moderately slow

Em G/D	D C	‖

VERSE 1

Em   G/D   D   C
Hello,   it's me,

Em   G/D   D   C
I was wondering if after all these years you'd like to meet

Em   G/D   D   C
to go over   everything.

Em   G/D   D   C
They say that times supposed to heal ya, but I ain't done much healing.

VERSE 2

Em   G/D   D   C
Hello,   can you hear me?

Em G/D   D   C
I'm in California dreaming about who we used to be

Em G/D   D   C
when we were younger   and free.

Em   G/D   D   C
I've forgotten how it felt before the world fell at our   feet.

PRE-CHORUS 1

Em   D Bm   C   Em D C
There's such a difference   between us and a million miles.

CHORUS

```
Em         C              G   D
Hello from the other side,

  Em             C                 G   D
I must've called a thousand times

        Em   C           G              D
to tell you     I'm sorry for everything that I've done,

            Em    C    G          D
but when I call     you never seem to be home.

Em         C          G   D
Hello from the outside,

  Em          C                G   D
at least I can say that I've tried

        Em   C       G          D
to tell you     I'm sorry for breaking your heart,

            Em   C         G          D
but it don't matter, it clearly doesn't tear you apart anymore.
```

INTERLUDE 1

```
| Em           G/D                    | D            C                    ||
```

VERSE 3

```
    Em   G/D      D      C
Hello,        how are you?

        Em   G/D        D        C
It's so typical of me to talk about myself, I'm sorry.

    Em   G/D            D   C
I hope        that you're well.

        Em        G/D              D       C
Did you ever make it out of that town where nothing ever happened?
```

PRE-CHORUS 2

```
        Em   D       Bm   C   Em   D   C
It's no secret   that the both of us are running out of time. So,
```

REPEAT CHORUS

INTERLUDE 2

```
Em  C     D   G
      Ooh,        anymore.

Em  C     D   G
      Ooh,        anymore.

Em  C     D   G         Em   C        D
      Ooh,        anymore.          Anymore.
```

REPEAT CHORUS

OUTRO

| Em   G/D | D   C | Em   ‖

I Drink Wine

Words and Music by Adele Adkins and Greg Kurstin

(Capo 3rd Fret)

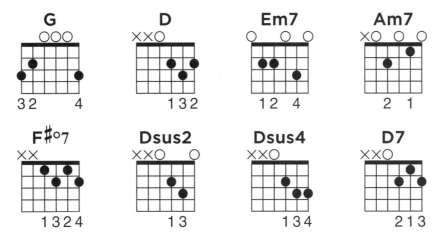

INTRO

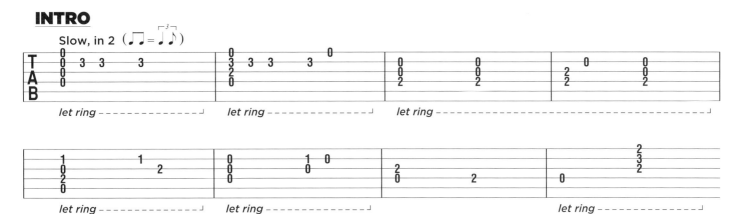

VERSE 1

```
        G                              D              Em7
How can one become so bounded by choices that somebody     else makes?

        G       Am7                    G              D
How come we've both     become a version of a person we don't even like?

        G                      D            Em7
We're in love  with the world but the world  just wants to bring us     down

        G   Am7                    G            D
by putting ideas     in or heads that corrupt  our hearts somehow.
```

VERSE 2

```
        G                    D                  Em7
When   I was a child every single thing could blow my     mind.

        G   Am7               G            D
Soaking it all     up for fun but now  I only soak up wine.

        G                      D                Em7
They say to play hard, you work hard, find balance in the sacrifice

        G   Am7               G        D
and yet I don't know     anybody who's truly satisfied.
```

PRE-CHORUS

```
                    G       F#°7           Em7      G
You better believe I'm trying, (trying,) to keep climbing (climbing)
```

```
        Am7                                    D   Dsus2   Dsus4   D7
but the higher we climb feels like we're both none the wiser. (Ah, ah.)      So, I hope I
```

CHORUS 1

```
    G         D   Em7
learn to get over myself,
```

```
            Am7   G           D
stop trying to be      somebody else.
```

```
            G         D     Em7
So we can love each other for      free,
```

```
            G      Am7   G          D
Everybody wants something, you just want   me.
```

VERSE 3

```
    G                   D               Em7
Why   am I obsessing about   the things I can't control?
```

```
        G   Am7           G              D
Why am I seeking approval from people I don't even know?
```

```
        G                 D             Em7
In these crazy times I hope to find something I can cling onto,
```

```
        G      Am7                      G                    D
'cause I need some substance in my life, something real, something that feels true.
```

PRE-CHORUS

```
                    G         F#°7         Em7   G
You better believe for you, I've cried,     (I've cried,) high tides, (high tides,)
```

```
        Am7                                         D   Dsus2   Dsus4   D7
'cause I want     you so bad but you can't fight fire with fire.   (Ah, ah.)      So, I hope
```

CHORUS 2

```
G         D   Em7
learn to get over myself,
```

```
            Am7   G           D
stop trying to be      somebody else.
```

```
                G          D     Em7
Oh, I just want to love you, love you   for free.
```

```
        G      Am7         G          D
Everybody wants something from me, you just want   me.
```

BRIDGE

```
         G                    D                 Em7
Listen, I know how low I can go, I give as good as I     get.

Am7                    G                        D
You get the brunt of it all 'cause you're all I've got  left.

         G              D                  Em7
Oh, I hope in time we both will find peace of mind.

                   Am7              G                     D    Dsus4   Dsus2
Sometimes the road     less traveled is a road best left behind.    Well,    I hope I
```

REPEAT CHORUS 2

```
                    G    D      Em7
You better believe I'm trying   to keep climbing

    G    Am7                 G                     D    Dsus4    D    Dsus2
but the higher we climb feels like   we're both none the wiser.
```

OUTRO

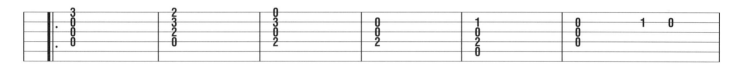

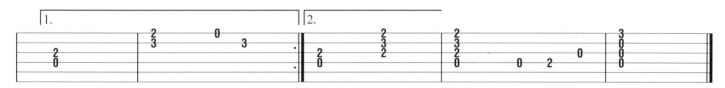

Love in the Dark

Words and Music by Adele Adkins and Samuel Dixon

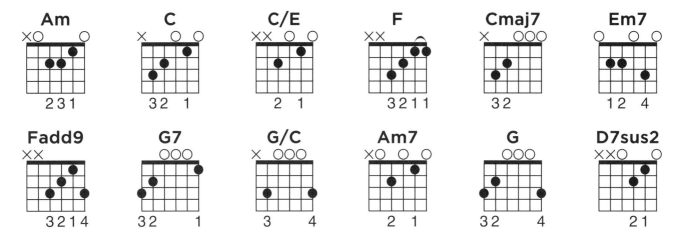

INTRO

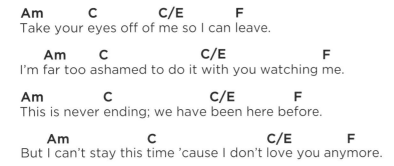

VERSE 1

Am   C   C/E   F
Take your eyes off of me so I can leave.

    Am   C   C/E   F
I'm far too ashamed to do it with you watching me.

Am   C   C/E   F
This is never ending; we have been here before.

    Am   C   C/E   F
But I can't stay this time 'cause I don't love you anymore.

PRE-CHORUS 1

    Am   Cmaj7   Em7   F
Please stay where you are, don't come any closer.

    Am   Cmaj7   Em7   F
Don't try to change my mind. I'm being cruel to be kind.

CHORUS

```
        Fadd9   G7          Am   G/C  C
I can't love     you in the dark.        It feels like we're

Fadd9   G7      Am   G/C  C
o  -    ceans apart.

          Fadd9         G7                  Am      G/C  C
There is so much space between us, baby, we're already defeated.

          Fadd9         G7          Am          G/C  C
Eh, eh, eh, eh, eh, eh, eh, eh, everything changed me.
```

VERSE 2

```
    Am          C           C/E         F
You have given me something that I can't live without.

    Am          C           C/E         F
You mustn't underestimate that when you are in doubt.

    Am          C           C/E         F
But I don't want to carry on like everything is fine.

    Am          C           C/E         F
The longer we ignore it all, the more that we will fight.
```

PRE-CHORUS 2

```
        Am      Cmaj7   Em7             F
Please don't fall apart, I can't face your breaking heart.

        Am      Cmaj7   Em7             F
I'm trying to be brave. Stop asking me to stay.
```

REPEAT CHORUS

BRIDGE

```
          Fadd9             G           Em7             Am7
We're not the only ones; I don't regret a thing. Every word I've said you know I'll always mean.

      Fadd9             G           D7sus2
It is the world to me that you are in my life, but I want to live and not just survive.
```

INTERLUDE

```
                                              |1.              |2.
‖: Fadd9        | G7        | Am        | G/C   C   :‖ G/C   C        ‖
                                                              That's why
```

REPEAT CHORUS

```
      Fadd9   G7              Am
And I         don't think you can save me.
```

Lovesong

Words and Music by Robert Smith, Laurence Tolhurst, Simon Gallup, Paul S. Thompson, Boris Williams and Roger O'Donnell

(Capo 3rd Fret)

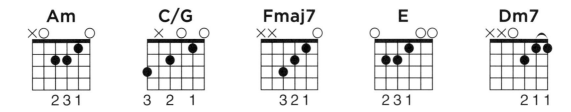

INTRO

VERSE 1

Am   C/G Fmaj7 E
Whenever I'm alone with you,

Am   C/G Fmaj7   E
you make me feel like I am home again.

Am   C/G Fmaj7 E
Whenever I'm alone with you,

Am   C/G Fmaj7   E
you make me feel like I am whole again.

INTERLUDE 1

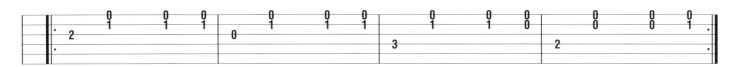

VERSE 2

Am   C/G Fmaj7 E
Whenever I'm alone with you,

Am   C/G Fmaj7   E
you make me feel like I am young again.

Am   C/G Fmaj7 E
Whenever I'm alone with you,

Am   C/G Fmaj7   E
you make me feel like I am fun again.

CHORUS 1

Fmaj7	Dm7	Am	C/G

However far away,   I will always love you.

Fmaj7	Dm7	Am	C/G

However long I stay,   I will always love you.

Fmaj7	Dm7	Am	C/G	Fmaj7	E

Whatever words I say,   I will always love you,   I will always love

INTERLUDE 2

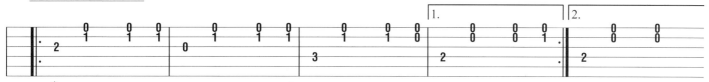

*you.
*First time only.

VERSE 3

Am	C/G	Fmaj7	E

Whenever I'm alone   with you,

Am	C/G	Fmaj7	E

you make me feel like I am free again.

Am	C/G	Fmaj7	E

Whenever I'm alone   with you,

Am	C/G	Fmaj7	E

you make me feel like I am clean again.

REPEAT CHORUS 1

GUITAR SOLO

*you.
*First time only.

CHORUS 2

Fmaj7	Dm7	Am	C/G

However far away,   I will always love you.

Fmaj7	Dm7	Am	C/G

However long I stay,   I will always love you.

Fmaj7	Dm7	Am	C/G	Fmaj7

Whatever words I say,   I will always love you,

E	Am	C/G	Fmaj7	E

I'll always love you,   I'll always love you.   'Cause I love

OUTRO

*you.
*First time only.

Make You Feel My Love

Words and Music by Bob Dylan

(Capo 1st Fret)

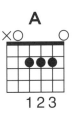
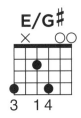
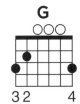
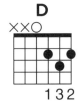

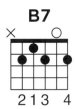

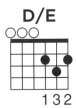
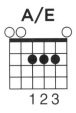
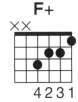
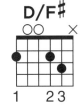
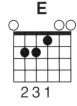
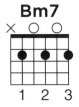
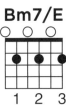

INTRO

Moderately slow

| A | E/G♯ | G | D | |
| Dm | A | B7   D/E | A | |

VERSE 1

A   E/G♯
When the rain is blowin' in your face,

G   D
and the whole world is on your case,

Dm   A
I could offer you a warm embrace

B7   D/E   A
to make you feel my love.

VERSE 2

A   E/G♯
When the evening shadows and the stars appear,

G   D
and there is no one there to dry your tears,

Dm   A
I could hold you for a million years

B7   D/E   A
to make you feel my love.

BRIDGE 1

D   A/E
  I know you haven't made your mind up yet,

F+   D/F♯   A
  but I would never do you wrong.

D   A
  I've known it from the moment that we met;

B7   E
no doubt in my mind where you belong.

VERSE 3

A   E/G♯
  I'd go hungry, I'd go black and blue.

G   D
  I'd go crawlin' down the avenue.

Dm   A
  Know there's nothing that I wouldn't do

B7   D/E   A
  to make you feel my love.

REPEAT INTRO

BRIDGE 2

D   A
  The storms are raging on the rollin' sea,

F+   D/F♯   A
  and on the highway of regret

D   A
  the winds of change are blowin' wild and free;

Bm7   Bm7/E
you ain't seen nothing like me yet.

VERSE 4

A   E/G♯
I could make you happy, make your dreams come true,

G   D
  nothing that I wouldn't do,

Dm   A
  go to the ends of the earth for you

B7   D/E   A
  to make you feel my love,

B7   D/E   A
  to make you feel my love.

Million Years Ago

Words and Music by Adele Adkins and Greg Kurstin

(Capo 4th Fret)

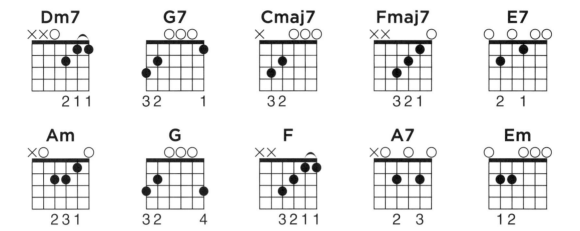

INTRO

Moderately

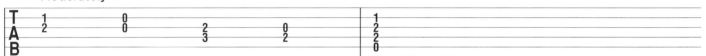

VERSE 1

Dm7   G7   Cmaj7   Fmaj7
I only wanted to have fun,   learning to fly, learning to run.

Dm7   E7   Am
I let my heart decide the way   when I was young.

A7   Dm7   G7   Cmaj7   Fmaj7
Deep down, I must have always known   that this woud be inevitable:

Dm7   E7
to earn my stripes I'd have to pay   and bear my

INTERLUDE 1

| Am | | G F | ‖: Am | | G F | :‖ E7 | | ‖
soul.

CHORUS

```
         Dm7              G7        Cmaj7              Fmaj7
I know I'm not the only one     who regrets the things they've done.

              Dm7          E7                    Am
Sometimes I just feel it's only me  ⎰who can't stand the reflec - tion     that     they    see.⎱
                                    ⎱who  nev - er became  who they thought they'd be.⎰

  A7      Dm7          G7        Cmaj7              Fmaj7
I wish I could live a little more,     look up to the sky, not just the floor.

         Dm7          E7            Am
I feel like my life is flashing by     and all I can do is watch and cry.

  A7      Dm7          G7            Cmaj7              Fmaj7
I miss the air, I miss my friends, I miss my mother, I miss it when

         Dm7                E7              Am  G   F    Em  Am
life was a party to be thrown,     but that was a mil - lion years a - go.
```

REPEAT INTRO

VERSE 2

```
              Dm7                G7        Cmaj7              Fmaj7
When I walk around all of the streets     where I grew up and found my feet,

         Dm7                E7                    Am
they can't look me in the eye,     it's like they're scared of me.

  A7    Dm7                G7        Cmaj7              Fmaj7
I try to think of things to say,     like a joke or a memory,

              Dm7                E7
but they don't recognize me now     in the light of
```

INTERLUDE 2

```
| Am          | G     F    ‖: Am          | G     F    :‖ E7          |            ‖
  day.
```

REPEAT CHORUS

```
  Am  G   F    Em  Am
A mil - lion years a - go.
```

Oh My God

Words and Music by Adele Adkins and Greg Kurstin

(Capo 1st Fret)

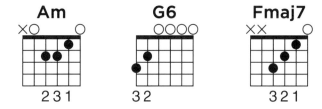

INTRO

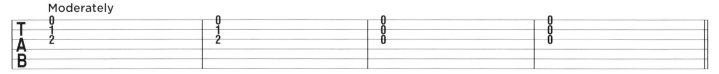

VERSE 1

Am
I ain't got too much time to spend

         G6
but I'll make time   for you to show how much I care.

Am
Wish that I would let you break my walls

        G6
but I'm still spinning out of control from the fall.

Am
Boy, you give good love, I won't lie,

        G6
it's what keeps me coming back even though I'm terrified.

PRE-CHORUS

Am
    I know that it's wrong but I want to have fun.

G6
    Mmm, yeah, mmm, yeah.

Fmaj7
    I know that it's wrong but I want to have fun.

G6
    Mmm, yeah, mmm, yeah.

CHORUS

Am

Oh,   my God, I can't believe it, out of all the people in the world,

G6

what   is the likelihood of jumping out of my life and into yours?

Fmaj7

Maybe, baby, I'm just losing my mind 'cause this is trouble, but it feels right,

G6

teetering on the edge of Heaven and Hell, it's a battle that I can not fight.

INTERLUDE

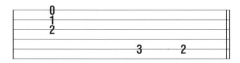

VERSE 2

Am

I'm a fool, but they all think I'm blind,

G6

I'd rather be   a fool than leave myself behind.

Am

I don't have to explain myself to you,

G6

I am a grown   woman and I do what I want to do.

REPEAT PRE-CHORUS

REPEAT CHORUS

BRIDGE

Am

(Lord, don't let me, I said, Lord, don't let me, I said, Lord, don't let me, let me down.)

G6

Oh, Lord,   don't   let   me   let   myself
   (Lord, don't let me, I said, Lord, don't let me,   I said, Lord, don't let me, let me down.)

Fmaj7

                          down.   Oh,   my,   God,
(Lord, don't let me, I said, Lord, don't let me, I said, Lord, don't let me, let me down.)

G6

 oh,   oh,   oh.
(Lord, don't let me, I said, Lord, don't let me, I said, Lord, don't let me, let me down.)

REPEAT CHORUS

OUTRO

Am

              I   know   that it's wrong   but I   want to have fun.

(Lord, don't let me, I said, Lord, don't let   me, I said, Lord, don't let me, let me down.)

G6

                 Mmm,   yeah,   mmm,   yeah.

(Lord, don't let me, I said, Lord, don't let me, I said, Lord, don't let me, let me down.)

Fmaj7

              I   know   that it's wrong   but I   want to have fun.

(Lord, don't let me, I said, Lord, don't let   me, I said, Lord, don't let me, let me down.)

G6

                 Mmm,   yeah,   mmm,   yeah.

(Lord, don't let me, I said, Lord, don't let me, I said, Lord, don't let me, let me down.)

One and Only

Words and Music by Adele Adkins, Dan Wilson and Greg Wells

(Capo 5th Fret)

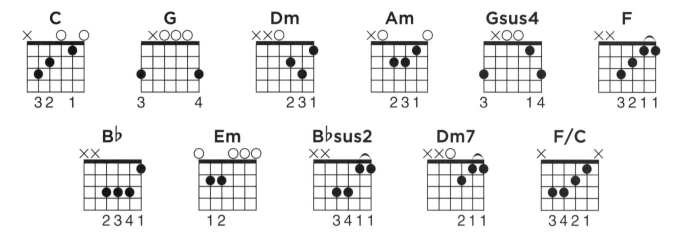

INTRO

Moderately slow

| C | | G | | ‖

VERSE 1

          C   G
You've been on my mind, I grow fonder every day,

          Dm   Am
Lose myself in time just thinking of your face.

G   C   G
God only knows why it's taken me so long

          Dm   Am   Gsus4 G
to let my doubts   go, you're the only one that I want.

PRE-CHORUS

          F   G   Am
I don't know why I'm scared, I've been here before,   Every feeling, every word, I've imagined it all.

B♭   F   Gsus4 G
You'll never know if you never try to forget your past and simply be mine.

CHORUS

```
           C                        Am
I dare you to let me be your, your one and only,

       Em                  F    Em   Dm      G
Promise I'm worthy to hold in your arms.    So come on    and give

C                          Am
me a chance to prove I am the one who can

       Em              F     Em  Dm  G
walk that mile until the end   starts.
```

VERSE 2

```
              C                 G
If I've been on your mind, you hang on every word I say,

       Dm         Am
Lose yourself in time at the mention of my name.

   G     C       G
Will I ever know how it feels to hold you close

         Dm              Am           Gsus4   G
and have you tell me, whichever road I choose you'll go?
```

REPEAT PRE-CHORUS

REPEAT CHORUS

INTERLUDE

```
| B♭sus2          |          | Dm7          |          |

| F/C             |          | F            |         ‖
```

BRIDGE

```
B♭sus2          Dm7
I know it ain't easy giving up your heart.

F/C           F
I know it ain't easy giving up your heart. Nobody's

B♭sus2          Dm7
perfect, trust me, I've learned it. Nobody's

F/C             F
perfect, trust me, I've learned it.

B♭sus2          Dm7
I know it ain't easy giving up your heart.

F/C            F           Gsus4   G
I know it ain't easy giving up your heart.    So,
```

OUTRO

```
(Dm)    (G)        C                                    Am
Come on      and give me a chance to prove I am the one who can

          Em                    F  Em        Dm   G   C
walk that mile until the end        starts.
```

Rolling in the Deep

Words and Music by Adele Adkins and Paul Epworth

(Capo 3rd Fret)

A5 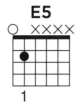 E5  G5   F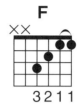

G 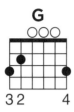 Am 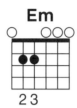 Em 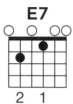 E7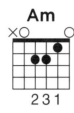

INTRO

Moderately

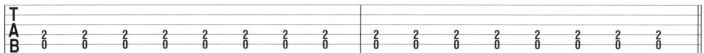

VERSE 1

A5   E5
There's a fire starting in my heart,

    G5   E5   G5
reaching a fever pitch and it's bringing me out the dark.

A5   E5
Finally, I can see you crystal clear.

    G5   E5   G5
Go ahead and sell me out and I'll lay your ship bare.

A5   E5
See how I leave with every piece of you,

    G5   E5   G5
don't underestimate the things that I will do.

A5   E5
There's a fire starting in my heart,

    G5   E5   G5
reaching a fever pitch and it's bringing me out the dark.

PRE-CHORUS 1

F   G   Em   F
The scars of your love remind me of us. They keep me thinking that we almost had it

          G   Em   E7
all. The scars of your love, they leave me breathless I can't help feeling: We could've had it

CHORUS 1

```
Am                          G
all.                                        Rolling in the
(You're gonna wish you, never had met me,

F                           G
deep.                   You      had my heart in -
tears are gonna fall, rolling in the deep.

Am                          G
side             of your hand                and you played
You're gonna wish you,           never had met me,

F                                           G
        it          to the beat.
tears are gonna fall,          rolling in the deep.)
```

VERSE 3

```
A5              E5
Baby, I have no story to be told.

     G5                          E5            G5
But I've heard one of you and I'm gonna make your head burn.

A5          E5
Think of me in the depth of your despair.

     G5                      E5          G5
Making a home down there as mine sure won't be shared.
```

PRE-CHORUS 2

```
F                                 G
            The    scars of your    love remind me
(You're gonna wish    you,         never had met   me,

Em                    F
 of      us. They  keep me thinking that we      almost had it
tears are gonna fall,          roll - ing in    the deep.

                              G
all.           The   scars of    your    love, they  leave me
You're gonna wish    you,        never had met    me,

Em                    E7
breath - less I    can't help feeling:  We      could've had it
tears are  gonna fall,          rolling in the deep.)
```

CHORUS 2

```
Am                          G
all.                                        Rolling in the
(You're gonna wish you, never had met me,

F                           G
deep.                   You      had my heart in -
tears are gonna fall, rolling in the deep.

Am                          G
side             of your hand                and you played
You're gonna wish you,           never had met me,

F                                           G
        it          to the beat.            Could've had it
tears are gonna fall,          rolling in the deep.)
```

BRIDGE

```
    F    G                  Am    G
    all.      Rolling in the deep.      You had my heart in -

    F                                    G
    side of your hand but you played    it with a beating.
```

VERSE 4

```
    N.C.
    Throw your soul through every open door.


    Count your blessings to find what you look for.

    A5                              G5
    Turn my sorrow into treasured gold.
           A5                                    G5
    You pay me back in kind and reap just what you sow.
```

BREAKDOWN

```
    Am                      G
                                      We      could've had it
    (You're gonna wish you, never had met      me,

    F                                G
    all,                    we       could've had it
    tears are gonna fall, rolling in the deep.

    Am                      G
    all,                                it
    You're gonna wish you, never had met me,

    F                                        G
    all,            it     all, it all.      We        could've had it
    tears are gonna fall,      rolling in the deep.)
```

REPEAT CHORUS 2

CHORUS 3

```
    Am                      G
    all.                                    Rolling in the
    (You're gonna wish you, never had met me,

    F                                G
    deep.                   You      had my heart in -
    tears are gonna fall, rolling in the deep.

    Am                              G
    side                    of your hand              but you played
    You're gonna wish you,              never had met me,

    F                              G       Am
       it, you played it, you played it, you played it to the beat.
```

Send My Love
(To Your New Lover)

Words and Music by Adele Adkins, Max Martin and Shellback

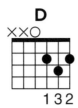
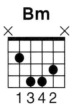

INTRO

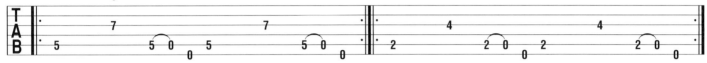

Moderately slow

VERSE 1

D

This was all you, none of it me. You put your hands on, on my body and

Bm

told me, mm, told me you were ready

D

for the big one, for the big jump, I'd be your last love, everlasting,

Bm

you and me. Mm, that was what you told me.

PRE-CHORUS

D

I'm giving you up, I've forgiven it all

Bm

You set me free.

CHORUS

D

Send my love to your new lover, treat her better.

Bm

We've gotta let go of all of our ghosts. We both know we ain't kids no more.

D

Send my love to your new lover, treat her better.

Bm

We've gotta let go of all of our ghosts. We both know we ain't kids no more.

INTERLUDE 1

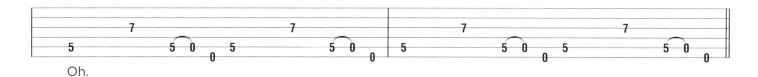

Oh.

VERSE 2

D
I was too strong, you were trembling, you couldn't handle the hot heat

Bm
rising, (rising) mm. Baby, I'm so rising.

D
I was running, you were walking, you couldn't keep up, you were falling

Bm
down, (down) mm. There's only one way down.

REPEAT PRE-CHORUS

REPEAT CHORUS

D
If you're ready, if you're ready, if you're ready, I'm ready.
(Oh.)

Bm
If you're ready, if you're ready. We both know we ain't kids no more.

INTERLUDE 2

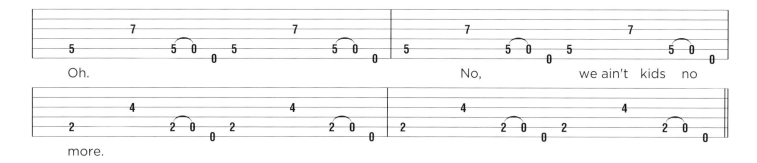

Oh.   No,   we ain't kids no

more.

REPEAT PRE-CHORUS

REPEAT CHORUS

OUTRO

D
Send my love   to your new lov - er,   treat   her bet - ter.
     (If you're read - y,   if you're ready, if you're read - y,   I'm ready.)

Bm
We've gotta let go of all of our ghosts. We both know we ain't kids no more.

D
Send my love   to your new lov - er,   treat   her bet - ter.
     (If you're read - y,   if you're ready, if you're read - y,   I'm ready.)

Bm   **N.C.**
We've gotta let go of all of our ghosts. We both know we ain't kids no more. Oh.

Set Fire to the Rain

Words and Music by Adele Adkins and Fraser Smith

(Capo 5th Fret)

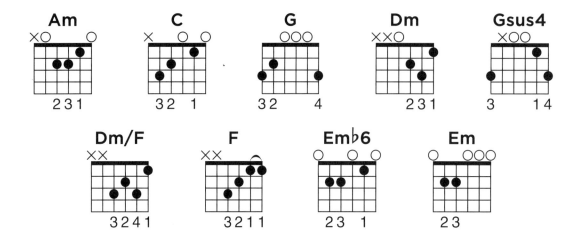

INTRO

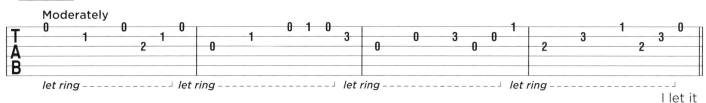

let ring - - - - - - - - - - - -   *let ring* - - - - - - - - - - - - - - - - - -   *let ring* - - - - - - - - - - - - - -   *let ring* - - - - - - - - - - - - - - - -

I let it

VERSE 1

Am   C   G   Dm
fall,   my heart. And as it fell you rose to claim it.

Am   C   G   Gsus4   G
It was dark and I was over until you kissed my lips and you saved me.

    Am   C   G   Dm
My hands, they were strong, but my knees were far too weak

    Am   C   G   Gsus4   G
to stand in your arms, without falling to your feet.   But there's a

PRE-CHORUS

Dm/F   Dm
side to you that I never knew, never knew,

        Am
all the things you'd say, they were never true, never true,

        F   G
and the games you'd play, you would always win, always win.

CHORUS 1

        Am   G
But I set fire to the rain, watched it pour as I touched your face.

        Dm   Am   G
well it burned while I cried, 'cause I heard it screaming out your name, your name.

VERSE 2

        Am   C   G   Dm
When laying with you, I could stay there, close my eyes,

        Am   C   G   Gsus4 G
feel you here forever, you and me together, nothing is better.   'Cause there's a

REPEAT PRE-CHORUS

CHORUS 2

        Am   G
But I set fire to the rain, watched it pour as I touched your face.

        Dm   Am   G
well it burned while I cried, 'cause I heard it screaming out your name, your name.

        Am   G
I set fire to the rain, and I threw us into the flames,

        Dm   F   G
well I felt something die 'cause I knew that that was the last time, the last time. (*Oh,)

                                                                                  *Last time only.

BRIDGE

              F   Em♭6   Em   G Gsus4 G
Sometimes I   wake up by the door, and heard you calling, must be waiting for   you,

              F   Em♭6   Em   G Gsus4 G
even now when we're already over, I can't help myself from looking for   you.

REPEAT CHORUS 2

OUTRO

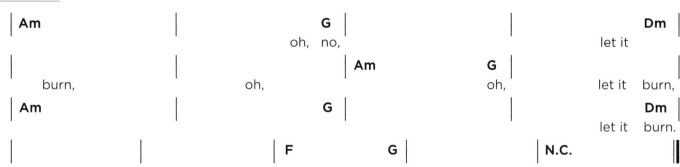

Skyfall

from the Motion Picture SKYFALL
Words and Music by Adele Adkins and Paul Epworth

(Capo 3rd Fret)

Am	F	Dm7	Am/B	Esus4
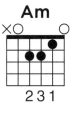	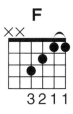	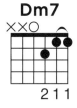	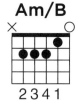	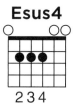
2 3 1	3 2 1 1	2 1 1	2 3 4 1	2 3 4

E	D7	Am/G	Am/E	F/C
		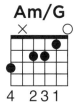	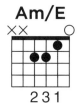	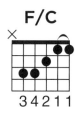
2 3 1	2 1 3	4 2 3 1	2 3 1	3 4 2 1 1

Bm7♭5	E7	D7sus2	Fmaj7	E7/G#
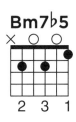		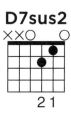	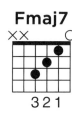	
2 3 1	2 1	2 1	3 2 1	2 3

INTRO

Moderately slow   *Play 3 times*

‖: Am   F | Dm7   :‖ Am/B | Esus4   E   ‖

This

VERSE 1

Am   F   Dm7
is the end.   Hold your breath and

Am   F   Dm7
count   to ten.   Feel the earth

Am   F   Dm7
move and then   hear my heart

Am/B   Esus4   E
burst   again.   For this

VERSE 2

Am   F   D7   Dm7
is the end.   I've drowned and dreamt this

Am   F   D7   Dm7
moment.   So overdue I

Am   F   D7   Dm7
owe them.   Swept away I'm

Am/B   Esus4   E
stol - en.   Let the

CHORUS

Am   Am/G   F   Am/E
sky fall. When it crumbles we will

Dm7   F/C   Bm7♭5   E7
stand tall, face it all   together. Let the

Am   Am/G   F   Am/E
sky fall. When it crumbles we will

D7   Bm7♭5   E7
stand tall, face it all together at sky -

INTERLUDE 1

| Am   F | D7   Dm7 | Am   F | D7   Dm7 ‖
fall.   At   sky -   fall.   Skyfall is

VERSE 3

Am   F   D7   Dm7
where we start,   a thousand miles and

Am   F   D7   Dm7
poles apart.   Where worlds collide and

Am   F   D7   Dm7
days are dark.   You may have my number, you can take my name

Am/B   Esus4   E
but you'll never have my heart.   Let the

REPEAT CHORUS

INTERLUDE 2

| Am | | | Am/G |
fall.   (Let the sky fall.)   (When it crumbles.)   (We will stand tall.)

| Am | | | ‖
    (Let the sky fall.)   (When it crumbles.)   (We will stand tall.)   Where you go

BRIDGE

D7sus2   Am/E   Fmaj7   Am/G   E7/G♯   Am   Am/G
I go. What you see, I see. I know I'll never be me   without the security of your

Fmaj7   Am/E   Dm7   Am   Am/B   E
loving arms keeping me from harm. Put your hand in my hand and we'll stand. Let the

REPEAT CHORUS

OUTRO

Am   Am/G   F   Am/E   Dm7   F/C   Bm7♭5   E7
fall. Let the sky fall.   We will stand tall   at sky -

Am   Am/G   F   Am/E   Dm7   E7/G♯   Am
fall.

Someone Like You

Words and Music by Adele Adkins and Dan Wilson

(Capo 2nd Fret)

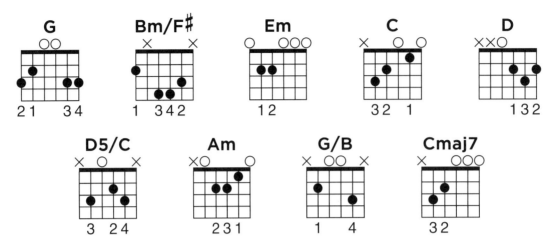

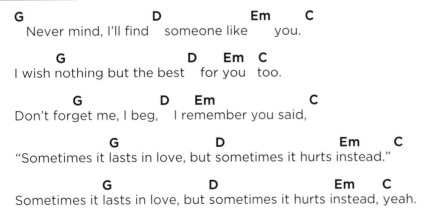

INTRO

Moderately slow

| G | | Bm/F# | | Em | | C | |

VERSE 1

G   Bm/F#   Em   C
I heard that you're settled down, that you found a girl and you're married now.

G   Bm/F#   Em   C
I heard that your dreams came true, guess she gave you things I didn't give to you.

G   Bm/F#   Em   C
Old friend, why are you so shy? Ain't like you to hold back or hide from the light.

PRE-CHORUS 1

D   Em   C
I hate to turn up out of the blue uninvited, but I couldn't stay away, I couldn't fight it.

D   Em   C   D5/C C
I had hoped you'd see my face and that you'd be reminded that for me, it isn't over.

CHORUS 1

G   D   Em C
 Never mind, I'll find someone like you.

G   D Em C
I wish nothing but the best for you too.

G   D Em   C
Don't forget me, I beg, I remember you said,

G   D   Em C
"Sometimes it lasts in love, but sometimes it hurts instead."

G   D   Em C
Sometimes it lasts in love, but sometimes it hurts instead, yeah.

VERSE 2

G   Bm/F♯   Em   C

You'd know how the   time flies, only   yesterday was the time of our lives.

           G   Bm/F♯   Em   C

We were born and raised in a   summer haze, bound by the surprise of our glory days.

PRE-CHORUS 2

D   Em   C

I hate to turn up out of the blue uninvited, but I   couldn't stay away, I couldn't fight it.

       D   Em   C   D5/C   C   D5/C

I had hoped you'd see my face and that you'd be reminded that for me, it isn't over.

CHORUS 2

G   D   Em   C

   Never mind, I'll find   someone like   you.

       G   D   Em   C

I wish nothing but the best   for you   too.

         G   D   Em   C

Don't forget me, I beg,   I remember you said,

             G   D   Em   C

"Sometimes it lasts in love, but sometimes it hurts instead."

BRIDGE

D   Em

Nothing compares, no worries or cares, regrets and mistakes, they are memories made.

C   Am   G/B   C   D5/C

Who would have known how bittersweet this would taste?

REPEAT CHORUS 2

REPEAT CHORUS 1

| D5/C   Cmaj7 | C | G |

To Be Loved

Words and Music by Adele Adkins and Tobias Jesso Jr.

(Capo 1st Fret)

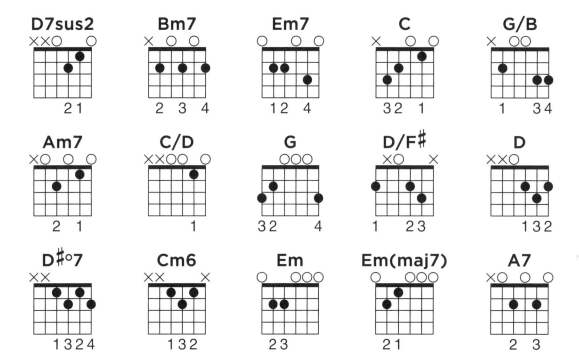

INTRO

VERSE 1

D7sus2   Bm7
I built a house for our love to grow,

            Em7
I was so young   that it was hard to know.

C   G/B
I'm as lost now as I   was back then,

Am7   C/D
always make a mess of   everything.

G   Bm7
It's about time that I face   myself,

           Em7
all I do is bleed   into someone else.

C   G/B
Painting walls with all my   secret tears,

Am7   C/D
filling rooms with all my   hopes and fears.

PRE-CHORUS

```
       G    D/F#      Em7    D
But oh,  my,     oh, my

                 C          G/B            Am7      C/D
I'll never learn if I never leap,     I'll always yearn if I never speak.
```

CHORUS 1

```
G        Bm7      C                      D
To be loved    and love  at the highest count, means to

Em7      G         C           D#°7
lose all the things I can't live without. Let it be known

    G    Bm7        C                    D
that I will choose to lose,   it's a sacrifice but I

Em7        G          C    Cm6             G    Bm7    C
can't live a lie.   Let it be known,   let it be known that I tried.
```

VERSE 2

```
    G                    Bm7
I'm   so afraid but I'm open wide,

             Em7
I'll be the one      to catch myself this time.

C                     G/B
  Tryin' to learn to lean      into it all,

Am7                   C/D
    ain't it funny how the      mighty fall?

G                    Bm7
  Looking back I don't regret a thing,

                       Em7
yeah, I took some bad turns       that I'm owning.

C                     G/B
  I'll stand still and let the storm pass by,

Am7                     C/D
    keep my heart safe 'til the time feels right.
```

REPEAT PRE-CHORUS

CHORUS 2

```
G        Bm7      C                      D
To be loved    and love  at the highest count, means to

Em7      G         C           D#°7
lose all the things I can't live without. Let it be known

    G    Bm7        C                    D
that I will choose to lose,   it's a sacrifice but I

Em7        G          C    Cm6
can't live a lie.   Let it be known,   let it be known that I
```

BRIDGE

```
Em   Em(maj7)                        G      A7
cried           for you. Even started lying     to you,

     Am7        Bm7     C          C/D
what a thing to do.       All   because I      wanted
```

CHORUS 3

```
G          Bm7         C                    D
to be loved      and love   at the highest count, means to

Em7        G          C           D#°7
lose all the things I can't live without. Let it be known, no, no,

   G     Bm7         C                     D
that I will choose, I will lose, it's a sacrifice but I

Em7         G         C        Cm6
can't live a lie.   Let it be known, let it be known that I
```

```
| G                 | Bm7              | C               |          D           |
  tried,                                                         that I
| Em7              | G                | C               | Cm6        N.C.      |
  tried,                                                Let  it be known       that I
|                  | G                |                 |                      ||
  tried.
```

When We Were Young

Words and Music by Adele Adkins and Tobias Jesso Jr.

(Capo 1st Fret)

Bm	D/F#	G	Em7	D	Asus4
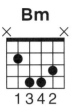	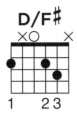	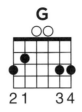	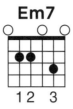	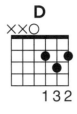	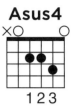
1 3 4 2	1 2 3	2 1 3 4	1 2 3	1 3 2	1 2 3

A	F#m	Gm	Em	F#7	D/A
	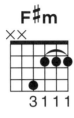	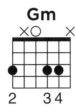	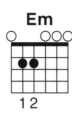	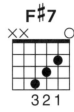	
1 2 3	3 1 1 1	2 3 4	1 2	3 2 1	1 3 2

INTRO

Moderately slow

| Bm   D/F# | G   D/F# | Em7 | | D | ‖

VERSE 1

Bm   D/F#   G D/F#   Em7   D
Everybody loves the things you do,   from the way you talk to the way you move.

Bm   D/F#   G D/F#   Em7   D
Everybody here is watching you,   'cause you feel like home, you're like a dream come true.

Bm   D/F#   G D/F#   Em7   D
But if by chance you're here alone,   can I have a moment before I go?

Bm   D/F#   G D/F#   Em7   Asus4   A
'Cause I've been by myself all night long,   hoping you're someone I used to know.

PRE-CHORUS 1

            G   A   F#m   G
You look like a movie,   you sound like a song;

              A   D/F#   Asus4
My God, this reminds me   of when we were young.

CHORUS 1

       D   D/F#   G   A
Let me photograph you in   this light, in case it is the last time

       D   D/F#   G   A
that we might be exactly like we were before we realized

         Bm   D/F#   G   Gm
we were sad of getting old, it made us restless.

         Em   Asus4   A
It was just like a movie, it was just like a song.

VERSE 2

Bm   D/F♯   G   D/F♯   Em7   D
I was so scared to face my fears,   'cause nobody told me that you'd be here.

Bm   D/F♯   G   D/F♯   Em7   Asus4 A
And I swore you moved overseas: that's what you said when you left me.

PRE-CHORUS 2

                  G   A   F♯m   G
You still look like a movie,   you sound like a song;

                        A   D/F♯ A
My God, this reminds me   of when we were young.

CHORUS 2

           D   D/F♯   G   A
Let me photograph you in   this light, in case it is the last time

           D   D/F♯   G   A
that we might be exactly like we were before we realized

           Bm   D/F♯   G   Gm
we were sad of getting old, it made us restless.

                Em   Asus4   F♯7
It was just like a movie, it was just like a song.

INTERLUDE 1

         Bm   D/A   G   D/F♯
When we   were young,   when we   were young,

         Em7   Asus4   F♯7
when we   were young, when we   were young.

 Bm   D/A   G   D/F♯
It's hard to win me back. Everything just takes me back to when

Em7   Asus4   F♯7
you were there, to when you were there.

      Bm   D/A   G   D/F♯
And a part of me keeps holding on just in case it hasn't gone.

      Em7   Asus4   A
I guess I still care. Do you still care?

PRE-CHORUS 3

                 G A   F♯m G
It was just like a movie,   it was just like a song;

                     A   F♯m A
My God, this reminds me   of when we were young.

INTERLUDE 2

```
  D   D/F#        G          A
     When we    were young,

           D           D/F#       G          A
When we    were young,      when we    were young,
```

CHORUS 3

```
          D              D/F#        G         A
Oh, let me photograph you in this light, in case it is the last time

          D       D/F#       G          A
that we might be exactly like we were before we realized

          Bm         D/F#       G      A
we were sad of getting old, it made us restless.

            Bm            D/F#         G       Gm
Woah, I'm so mad I'm getting old, it makes me reckless.

                Em                   Asus4   A
It was just like a movie, it was just like a song.

                 D
When we were young.
```

Turning Tables

Words and Music by Adele Adkins and Ryan Tedder

(Capo 3rd Fret)

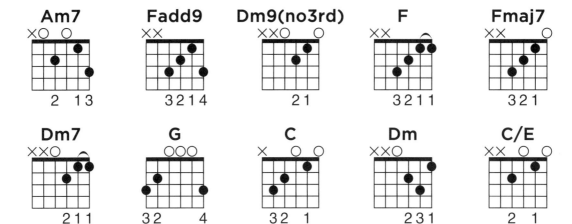

INTRO

Moderately slow

| Am7 | Fadd9 | Dm9(no3rd) | F   Fmaj7 | ||

VERSE 1

Am7   Fadd9   Dm9(no3rd)   F   Fmaj7
Close enough to start a war,   all that I have is on the floor.

Am7   Fadd9   Dm9(no3rd)   F   Fmaj7
God only knows what we're fighting for,   all that I say, you always say more.

PRE-CHORUS

F   Fmaj7   Dm7
I can't keep up with your turning tables, under

F   Fmaj7   G
your thumb, I can't breathe.

CHORUS 1

   Am7   Fmaj7 C   Dm
So, I won't let you close enough to hurt me,

    Am7   FmaJ7   C   Dm
no, I won't ask you, you to just desert me.

      Am7   Fmaj7 F   C/E   G
I can't give you   what you think you gave me.

        Dm7 C   Fadd9   Am7 Fadd9   Dm9(no3rd) F Fmaj7
It's time to say   goodbye to turning tables,   to turning tables.

VERSE 2

  Am7   Fadd9 Dm9(no3rd)   F   Fmaj7
   Under haunted skies, I see, ooh,   where love is lost, your ghost is found.

  Am7   Fadd9
   I've braved a hundred storms   to leave you, as hard as you

Dm9(no3rd)   F   Fmaj7
try, no, I will never be knocked down.

REPEAT PRE-CHORUS

REPEAT CHORUS 1

BRIDGE

Am7   Fmaj7   C   Dm
Next time I'll be braver, I'll be my own saviour when thunder calls for me.

Am7   Fmaj7   C   G
Next time I'll be braver, I'll be my own saviour standing on my own two feet.

CHORUS 2

Am7   Fmaj7 C   Dm
I won't let you close enough to hurt me,

  Am7   Fmaj7 C   Dm
no, I won't ask you, you to just desert me.

    Am7   Fmaj7 F   C/E   G
I can't give you   what you think you gave me.

      Dm7 C Fadd9   Am7 Fadd9   Dm9(no3rd) F Fmaj7
It's time to say   goodbye to turning tables,   to turning tables.   Turning

Am7   Fadd9   Dm9(no3rd) F   Am7
tables, yeah,   ta - da, na, no,   yeah.

Water Under the Bridge

Words and Music by Adele Adkins and Gregory Kurstin

(Capo 3rd Fret)

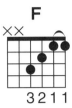   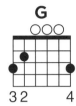  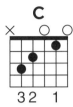

INTRO

Moderately slow

| F   Dm7 | | Am   G | C/E ||

VERSE 1

```
      F              Dm7      Am              G        C/E
If you're not the one for me,   then I'll come, I can bring you to your knees.

      F              Dm7      Am              G      C/E
If you're not the one for me,   why do I hate the idea of being free?

      F                  Dm7              Am                  G  C/E
And if I'm not the one for you,   you've gotta stop holding me the way you do.  Oh,

         F            Dm7           Am                              G        C/E
honey, if I'm not the one for you,   why have we been through what we have been through?  It's so
```

PRE-CHORUS 1

```
F  Dm7          Am  G   C/E
cold out here in your wilderness.  I want

F           Dm7      Am                      G
you to be my keeper, but not if you are so reckless.
```

CHORUS 1

```
N.C.          C                       Dm7
If you're gonna let me down, let me down gently. Don't pretend that you don't want me.

Am                       F
Our love ain't water under the bridge.

              C                       Dm7
If you're gonna let me down, let me down gently. Don't pretend that you don't want me.

Am                       F
Our love ain't water under the bridge.

     C   Dm7       Am                      F
Oh, woah,       say that our love ain't water under the bridge.
```

VERSE 2

  F   Dm7   Am   G   C/E
What are you waiting for? You never seem to make it through the door.

     F   Dm7   Am   G   C/E
And who are you hiding from? It ain't no life to live like you're on the run.

     F   Dm7   Am   G
Have I ever asked for much? The only thing that I want is your love.

REPEAT CHORUS 1

PRE-CHORUS 2

     F   Dm7   Am G   C/E
It's so cold out here in your wilderness. I want

F   Dm7   Am   G
you to be my keeper, but not if you are so reckless.

CHORUS 2

N.C.   C   Dm7
If you're gonna let me down, let me down gently. Don't pretend that you don't want me.

Am   F
Our love ain't water under the bridge.

                  C   Dm7
If you're gonna let me down, let me down gently. Don't pretend that you don't want me.

Am   F
Our love ain't water under the bridge.

     C   Dm7
Oh, woah,   say that
    (Say it ain't so, say it ain't so, say it ain't so, say it ain't so,

Am   F
our   love ain't water   under the bridge.   Oh,
say it ain't so,   say it ain't   so, say it ain't so, say it ain't so.
C   Dm7
woah,   say that
Say it ain't so, say it ain't so, say it ain't so, say it ain't so.

Am   F
our   love ain't water   under the bridge.   Oh,
say it ain't so,   say it ain't   so, say it ain't so, say it ain't so.)
C Dm7   Am N.C.
       Say that our love ain't water under the bridge.

Woman Like Me

Words and Music by Adele Adkins and Dean Josiah Cover

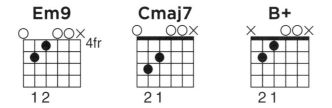

INTRO

Moderately

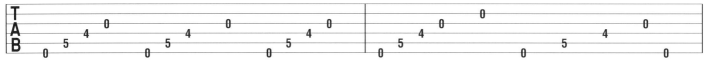

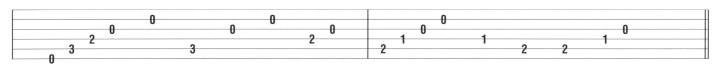

You're driv -

VERSE 1

Em9
  - ing me away, give me a reason to stay.

Cmaj7   **B+**
I want to be lost in you, but not in this way.

Em9
I don't think you quite understand who you have on your hands.

Cmaj7   **B+**
How can you not see just how good for you I am?

Em9
I know that you've been hurt before, that's why you feel so insecure.

Cmaj7   **B+**
I begged you to let me in 'cause I only want to be the cure.

Em9
If you don't choose to grow, we ain't ever gonna know

Cmaj7   **B+**
just how good this could be. I really hope that this would go

Em9   **Cmaj7** **B+**
somewhere.

CHORUS 1

      Em9   Cmaj7   B+
Complacency is the worst trait to have, are you crazy? You ain't ever had, ain't ever had a woman like

Em9   Cmaj7   B+
    me. It is so sad a man like you could be so lazy.

      Em9   Cmaj7   B+
Consistency is the gift to give for free and it is   key to ever keep, to ever keep a woman

Em9   Cmaj7   B+
    like me.

VERSE 2

      Em9
All you do is complain about decisions you make.

      Cmaj7   B+
How can I help lift you if you refuse to activate the life

Em9
that you truly want? I know it's hard, but it's not.

         Cmaj7   B+
We come from the same place, but you will never give it up.

         Em9
It's where they make you feel powerful, that's why you think I make you feel small.

         Cmaj7   B+
But that's you projection, it's not my rejection.

        Em9
I put my heart on the line for the very first time

         Cmaj7   B+
because you asked me to and now you've gone and changed your mind.

        Em9
But loving you was a breakthrough, I saw what my heart can really do.

        Cmaj7   B+
Now some other man will get the love I have for you 'cause you don't

Em9   Cmaj7 B+
    care. Oh, oh.

CHORUS 2

Em9   Cmaj7   B+
Complacency is the worst trait to have, are you crazy? You ain't ever had, ain't ever had a woman like

Em9   Cmaj7   B+
 me. It is so sad a man like you could be so lazy.

Em9   Cmaj7   B+
Consistency is the gift to give for free and it is   key to ever keep, to ever keep a woman

Em9   Cmaj7 B+
 like me. A woman like   me.

Em9
Complacency   is the worst trait I have,
    (Woman like me.)

Cmaj7   B+
are you crazy?   You ain't ever had, ain't ever had a woman like
    (Woman like   me.)

Em9   Cmaj7   B+
 me. It is so sad a man like you could be so lazy.

       Em9
 Con - sis - ten - cy   is the gift to give for free
(Woman like me. Woman like me.)
                    Fade out
Cmaj7   B+   Em9
and it is   key. To ever keep, to ever keep a woman like me.

GUITAR NOTATION LEGEND

Chord Diagrams

CHORD DIAGRAMS graphically represent the guitar fretboard to show correct chord fingerings.

- The letter above the diagram tells the name of the chord.
- The top, bold horizontal line represents the nut of the guitar. Each thin horizontal line represents a fret. Each vertical line represents a string; the low E string is on the far left and the high E string is on the far right.
- A dot shows where to put your fret-hand finger and the number at the bottom of the diagram tells which finger to use.
- The "O" above the string means play it open, while an "X" means don't play the string.

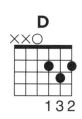

Tablature

TABLATURE graphically represents the guitar fingerboard. Each horizontal line represents a string, and each number represents a fret.

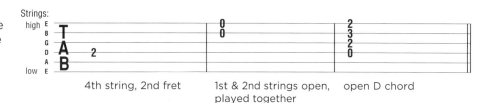

4th string, 2nd fret   1st & 2nd strings open, played together   open D chord

Definitions for Special Guitar Notation

HAMMER-ON: Strike the first (lower) note with one finger, then sound the higher note (on the same string) with another finger by fretting it without picking.

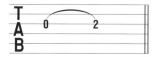

PULL-OFF: Place both fingers on the notes to be sounded. Strike the first note and without picking, pull the finger off to sound the second (lower) note.

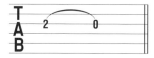

LEGATO SLIDE: Strike the first note and then slide the same fret-hand finger up or down to the second note. The second note is not struck.

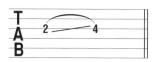

SHIFT SLIDE: Same as legato slide, except the second note is struck.

Additional Musical Definitions

N.C. •No chord. Instrument is silent.

•Repeat measures between signs.

REALLY EASY GUITAR

Easy-to-follow charts to get you playing right away are presented in these collections of arrangements in chords, lyrics and basic tab for all guitarists.

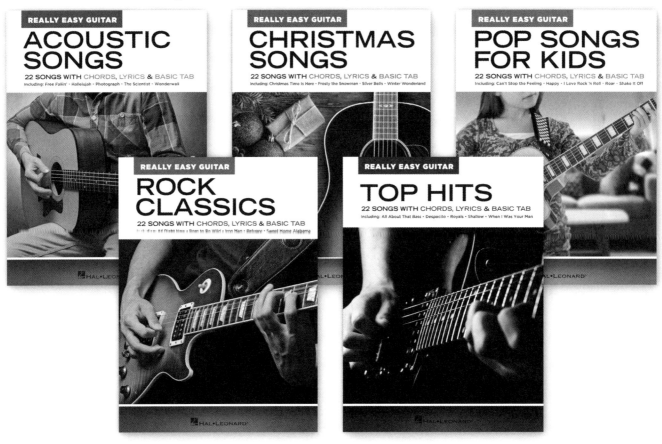

ACOUSTIC CLASSICS
22 songs: Angie • Best of My Love • Dust in the Wind • Fire and Rain • A Horse with No Name • Layla • More Than a Feeling • Night Moves • Patience • Time in a Bottle • Wanted Dead or Alive • and more.
00300600 .... $9.99

ACOUSTIC SONGS
22 songs: Free Fallin' • Good Riddance (Time of Your Life) • Hallelujah • I'm Yours • Losing My Religion • Mr. Jones • Photograph • Riptide • The Scientist • Wonderwall • and more.
00286663 ....$10.99

ADELE
22 songs: All I Ask • Chasing Pavements • Daydreamer • Easy On Me • Hello • I Drink Wine • Love in the Dark • Lovesong • Make You Feel My Love • Turning Tables • Water Under the Bridge • and more.
00399557 ....$12.99

THE BEATLES FOR KIDS
14 songs: All You Need Is Love • Blackbird • Good Day Sunshine • Here Comes the Sun • I Want to Hold Your Hand • Let It Be • With a Little Help from My Friends • Yellow Submarine • and more.
00346031..$10.99

CHRISTMAS CLASSICS
22 Christmas carols: Away in a Manger • Deck the Hall • It Came upon the Midnight Clear • Jingle Bells • Silent Night • The Twelve Days of Christmas • We Wish You a Merry Christmas • and more.
00348327.. $9.99

CHRISTMAS SONGS
22 holiday favorites: Blue Christmas • Christmas Time Is Here • Frosty the Snowman • Have Yourself a Merry Little Christmas • Mary, Did You Know? • Silver Bells • Winter Wonderland • and more.
00294775.. $9.99

THE DOORS
22 songs: Break on Through to the Other Side • Hello, I Love You (Won't You Tell Me Your Name?) • L.A. Woman • Light My Fire • Love Her Madly • People Are Strange • Riders on the Storm • Touch Me • and more.
00345890 .... $9.99

BILLIE EILISH
14 songs: All the Good Girls Go to Hell • Bad Guy • Everything I Wanted • Idontwannabeyouanymore • No Time to Die • Ocean Eyes • Six Feet Under • Wish You Were Gay • and more.
00346351 ....$10.99

POP SONGS FOR KIDS
22 songs: Brave • Can't Stop the Feeling • Happy • I Love Rock 'N Roll • Let It Go • Roar • Shake It Off • We Got the Beat • and more.
00286698..$10.99

ROCK CLASSICS
22 songs: All Right Now • Born to Be Wild • Don't Fear the Reaper • Hey Joe • Iron Man • Old Time Rock & Roll • Refugee • Sweet Home Alabama • You Shook Me All Night Long • and more.
00286699 ....$10.99

TAYLOR SWIFT
22 hits: Back to December • Cardigan • Exile • Look What You Made Me Do • Mean • The One • Our Song • Safe & Sound • Teardrops on My Guitar • We Are Never Ever Getting Back Together • White Horse • You Need to Calm Down • and more.
00356881..$10.99

TOP HITS
22 hits: All About That Bass • All of Me • Despacito • Love Yourself • Royals • Say Something • Shallow • Someone like You • This Is Me • A Thousand Years • When I Was Your Man • and more.
00300599 .... $9.99

halleonard.com